Table of Contents

Other Books by Jennif...	5
Introduction to the Wo...	7
A Green Smoothie Exp...	9
Are Green Smoothies Good for Me?	10
How Does a Smoothie Differ from Juicing?	13
TECHNIQUES FOR SUCCESSFUL GREEN SMOOTHIES	15
What is the Basic Formula for a Smoothie?	17
Invest in Good Equipment	20
Some Helpful Blender Tips	21
What Greens Should I Use in My Smoothies?	23
Other Vegetables to Experiment with in Your Smoothies	25
What Are Some Good Fruits to Use in My Smoothies?	27
What Other Ingredients Can I Add to My Smoothie?	29
How to Buy, Clean, Store and Even FREEZE Your Produce	35
Washing Your Greens	36
No-Wash Method for Your Greens	37
Freezing Your Greens	38
Why Freeze Greens?	39
Freezing Your Fruits	40
TIPS AND TRICKS OF GREEN SMOOTHIE MAKING	43
Helpful Tips and Tricks	45
Let's Drink!	51
SMOOTHIE RECIPES	53
New Beginnings Smoothie	54
Simple Smoothie	55
Polynesian Smoothie	55
Spicy Raspberry Smoothie	55
Fruity Spinach Smoothie	56
Orangana Pear Smoothie	56

Green Goddess Smoothie	57
Frosty Green Smoothie	57
Sweet Goodness Smoothie	57
Nutty Green Smoothie	58
Bunny's Favorite Smoothie	58
Green Coconut Smoothie	58
Berry Good Smoothie	59
CinnaPear Smoothie	60
Green Pines Smoothie	60
Nutty Banana Smoothie	60
Dark and Delicious Smoothie	61
Applelicious Smoothie	62
CocoPiney Smoothie	62
Smoothy Smoothie	63
Berry Springy Smoothie	63
Apple Peary Smoothie	64
Red Chalet Smoothie	64
Refreshing Strawberry Smoothie	64
Luscious Pink Smoothie	65
Purple Passion Smoothie	65
Hawaiian Smoothie	66
Grapes Nuts Smoothie	66
Blueberry Delight Smoothie	67
Mixed Up Smoothie	67
Green Banana Smoothie	68
Green Refreshment Smoothie	68
Blue Heaven Smoothie	68
INDEX OF RECIPE INGREDIENTS	69
About the Author	78

Other Books by Jennifer Wells

Going Gluten Free: A Quick Start Guide for a Gluten-Free Diet

Gluten-Free Kids: A Quick Start Guide for a Healthy Kids Diet

Juice for Health: Juice Fasting for Health and Wellness

Top 10 Tips to Help You Lose Weight

A Quick Start Guide to Beginning Yoga

Introduction to the World of the Green Smoothie

Are you searching for a healthy way to start your day? Have you been trying to discover nutritious snacks? Well, a green smoothie could be just what you are looking for. Whether you are new to the world of green smoothies or a seasoned veteran, green smoothies are some of the tastiest and easiest ways to bring more nutrition and delicious flavors into your day.

As you read this material I've put together for you in this book, you will learn some valuable tidbits about green smoothies, yet I promise not to overwhelm you with too much information. In fact, I want to make this book as user-friendly as possible. I have included some data that will help you if you are new to this form of nutrition, yet I have tried to spare you all the "mumbo-jumbo" about green smoothies you will find in the scientific publications and magazines available in the marketplace.

The Green Smoothie: A Quick Start Guide is exactly what it claims to be – a quick start guide. I want you to get excited about learning the basics of how to make delicious smoothies so you can get started as soon as you are ready so you can experience the benefits of the recipes you'll find in the second half of my book.

I want to share with you what green smoothies are; what kinds of vegetables and fruits you can use in them; how to buy, clean, store, and even freeze greens and fruits; and some delicious recipes you can make, often with ingredients you already have in your kitchen.

My book does not focus on one particular lifestyle choice like gluten-free, dairy-free, paleo, or vegetarian. However, I've tried to concentrate on using healthy ingredients that are not difficult to obtain, as well as challenging you to try ones that may be new to you.

While green smoothies have been shown to be instrumental in weight loss, I will not try and convince you or provide a diet plan for trying to lose weight. My purpose is to get you excited about how to make them so that you will enjoy drinking them. Once you do and start incorporating them into your daily routine, then you can read other books on how to use them as a diet plan. I want you to remember my book as one that helped you create a "lifestyle" of enjoying green smoothies—not just a diet.

Now, let me take you briefly through a "crash course" that focuses on the wonderful health benefits you will taste and experience in the culinary world of green smoothies!

A Green Smoothie Explained

I like to tell people that green smoothies are vegetables that taste so good that you should not have much trouble convincing your children to drink them! My goal is to help you discover for yourself why green smoothies are not only some of the healthiest drinks you can have, but that they can taste great, too. All you really have to do is take the time to learn the "3 T's" – some basic Techniques, Tips and Tricks.

Begin by thinking of "greens" as the combination of two different categories. For example, you have the leaves of a plant that are attached to a stem like lettuces that are quite flexible and flat. Then you have vegetables like celery and broccoli. These are often flexible enough that you could wrap them around your finger. Blending green vegetables like celery, broccoli, and spinach with fruits such as mangoes, bananas, and apples makes a green smoothie incredibly nutritious and allows for unlimited taste combinations.

Additionally, it is the nutritious "greens" that give green smoothies their color. Yet, not all green smoothies are green! Sometimes a green smoothie will be brown or purple because of fruits like blackberries and blueberries added to the leafy vegetables.

For the purposes of this book, we are going to consider "green" as something nutritious, yet even this has many variables to it. For instance, if you have not eaten well in the past, for you, "green" will mean simply learning to eat healthier. This may be as simple as incorporating fresh fruits and vegetables into your diet instead of the canned fruits, junk foods and fast foods that have previously constituted a large part of your diet.

Yet, for those of you who have regularly eaten fresh fruits and vegetables, "green" for you may mean adding more organics and healthier ingredients into your diet than you used to.

A basic "formula" for creating a good tasting green smoothie would be to include 2 big handfuls or 2 cups of firmly-packed greens with two or three fruits. This means your smoothie might include 2 cups of baby spinach or romaine lettuce along with a banana, some pineapple and berries—enough fruit to give the smoothie the juiciness and smoothness you want and the sweetness to offset the greens as well.

With a combination like this, the taste of the green vegetables is lost and the smoothie will taste fruity and sweet. In addition, to balance the taste of this type of smoothie, you can use fruits that have stronger flavors like mangoes and pineapples instead of bananas, cherries and grapes. Be assured that after you get the hang of it, you won't worry too much about measurements—you'll get to where you can guestimate how much of each to put in for good tasting smoothies because of past experiences.

Learning to make and enjoy drinking green smoothie will mean different things to different people. However, no matter where you are in your journey, green smoothies have some definite health benefits that I will cover briefly in the next section.

Are Green Smoothies Good for Me?

You bet they are! With healthy, vitamin-rich foods like spinach, kale, celery, and fruits, smoothies are a great way to take in many nutrients from the veggies and fruits as you drink. In addition, because you can get a lot of vegetables and fruits crunched up inside a smoothie, you actually can "drink" more of these nutritious foods than you would normally be able to eat in the same meal.

For many just beginning to venture into the world of green smoothies, this "new" drink may take some getting used to. Drinking leafy greens, as well as other vegetables, may prove to be a challenge to you starting out. Leaning heavily toward added fruits and healthy sweeteners may help your taste buds in the beginning. You may have a palette that requires some time to get used to the taste of vegetable juices. I will have more on how to get started as a beginner later in the recipes section.

At this point, I want to list numerous reasons why green smoothies are good for you to get you excited and inspired to try them if you never have, and to motivate you if you haven't made them in awhile. Although they may sound rather technical, they are worth knowing.

1. Many of the greens used in smoothies are dark, leafy vegetables that are known to be rich in zinc, potassium, calcium, iron, magnesium, and phosphorus. They are also loaded with amino acids.

2. Greens are often used in combination with a healthy fat like coconut oil, avocados, and olive oil. By combining these, good fats help to deliver vitamins and minerals to different parts of your body so they can be absorbed easily.

3. Including dark, leafy greens in your diet can improve the functions of your immune system, improve kidney and liver function, and help elevate the number of healthy intestinal flora for a healthier digestive system.

4. One cup of these greens offers valuable supplies of vitamins K, E, and C, as well as beta-carotene, folic acid, fiber, and many other nutrients and minerals.

5. Many testify that green smoothies seem to lift their spirits and help them fight off depression. Maybe it is because they know they are doing something healthy for their bodies.

6. Green smoothies are satisfying and cause you to feel full. This often helps people to keep from indulging in excessive eating after they drink them. Many attest to the fact that they lose weight when they regularly drink green smoothies.

7. Ingredients used in smoothies help you maintain a healthy digestive system and strengthen your immune system. In addition, they supply generous amounts of vitamins, minerals, and liquids to keep your digestive system working efficiently.

8. Fruits and vegetables in green smoothies often contain agents that fight against cancer, minimize the development of heart disease, and power up your immune system.

9. Adding a green smoothie to your diet has been shown to help reduce sugar cravings. This is also another reason attributed to people's ability to lose weight.

10. Because smoothies have a high raw vegetable content, they are reported to help speed up your digestive process and allow you to experience renewed energy.

11. When greens are combined with fruits, the fiber in the greens actually helps to slow down your body's absorption rate of the sugar from the fruit.

12. Be advised ~ Ingredients like carrots and bananas in your smoothies, along with fruits with a lot of natural sugars (pineapple, watermelon, etc.) can raise your blood sugar. If you are diabetic, this is something you definitely need to seek the counsel of your health care professional before starting a regimen of green smoothies.

13. Finally, a green smoothie is probably the healthiest "fast food" there is!

How Does a Smoothie Differ from Juicing?

Smoothies and juicing offer many of the same wonderful qualities when it comes to healthy nutritious benefits your body will enjoy. However, there are some differences that exist between how they are created, their consistencies and textures, and a few tidbits.

Let me start with juicing since I've certainly done my share of this as well. (If you would like to know even more about juicing than what you will learn here, you can read my book called, ***Juice for Health: Juice Fasting for Health and Wellness***)

Juices

Juices are essentially the liquid content of a fruit or plant. Through extraction, the juice becomes separated from the plant's pulp, resulting in the juice's absence of fiber and any solids.

Preparation

A juice extractor is used to "squeeze" the juice from a plant or fruit. Squeezing the fruit with your hands can accomplish this; however, it is almost impossible to create juice from vegetables with your hands. As a result, a powerful juicing machine is recommended to effectively make healthy and nutritious juices from vegetables and fruits. Using a good quality-juicing machine allows you to drop many fruits and vegetables right into the hopper without having to cut, chop or squeeze.

Consistency

Because the pulp and fiber of fruits and vegetables have been removed, the juice is quite thin—almost water-like in its consistency. Many juices even have a translucent appearance whereas a smoothie does not.

Health Benefits

Juices are extremely effective at hydrating your body and do not require much effort on the part of your digestive system. The nutrients from the juices are quickly absorbed into your bloodstream and can be quite effective at boosting your energy levels.

Smoothies

Smoothies are literally drinks created by blending numerous ingredients together in a high-speed blender. All the pulp and fiber of the ingredients are blended together with the juices of the fruits and vegetables—they are not separated in any way.

Preparation

A blender or smoothie maker is required to prepare this drink. All you need is a good blender that mixes all the ingredients together, allowing you to enjoy a drink that can taste great and is full of the nutrients and fiber from fruits and vegetables.

Texture

Smoothies are thicker than juices because they contain all the fiber and pulp of the fruits and vegetables blended together. They usually have a smooth, creamy texture and are not translucent like juices are.

Health Benefits

Smoothies and especially green smoothies are associated with many health benefits, as I have shared with you previously. They aid in weight loss and digestion that is more effective. By enhancing your body's metabolism, they boost your energy levels. Some people find that when they drink green smoothies, they experience detoxifying characteristics that improve the quality of their hair, nails and skin.

I hope this gives you a better idea of the similarities and differences between these two types of healthy and nutritious beverages. Personally, I enjoy doing a combination of both juicing and green smoothies. It gives me enough variety of flavors, textures, and nutrients—all while enjoying the benefits of healthy drinks.

TECHNIQUES FOR SUCCESSFUL GREEN SMOOTHIES

What Is the Basic Formula for a Smoothie?

Before I take you into the discussions of what greens to use, what fruits are good, and what additional ingredients work well in a smoothie, I want to give you the basic "formula" for making green smoothies. If you can see a green smoothie from "50,000 feet," you will feel empowered and will not be afraid to create your own smoothie recipes in the future.

There are six different steps to process and go through when making a smoothie. Some steps are optional but are often incorporated—depending upon your tastes, availability, and budget.

Step 1: Pick a fluid ~ Every smoothie will need some type of liquid in it. You will use anywhere from 1½ cups to 2 cups of liquid. (You will want the liquid added first so your blender can mix ingredients up effectively.)

Step 2: Add some greens ~ A smoothie usually has about 2 cups or 1 big handful of greens added to it. These go in on top of the liquid.

Step 3: Add some fruit ~ Fruits add sweetness and texture. You will add about 2 cups of fruit that can be fresh or frozen (Using frozen fruit is especially nice if you like a frosty smoothie like me.)

Step 4: Add a superfood or two (optional) ~ Superfoods are ingredients that are not necessary, but can add additional nutritional content to your smoothie.

Step 5: Sweeten your smoothie (optional) ~ Sometimes the taste of your smoothie may be stronger than you like. Adding a little sweetness could make it more palatable and enjoyable.

Step 6: Turn on the blender ~ Blend up the ingredients until they have the desired consistency. While your smoothie is still in the blender, you can add ice to thicken it, liquid to thin it out, or sweetness if desired. Just be sure to taste it with your finger before you pour it.

Step 7: Drink and enjoy! (Just thought I'd throw in a 7th step for fun!)

On the next page you will find a helpful chart you can refer to for easy reference with some suggestions of foods you can include in your smoothie. While not an exhaustive list of ingredients, it's enough to get you going.

Steps for Creating a Green Smoothie

Step 1: Pick a fluid: (about 1½ cups)

Coconut water	Nut milks
Rice milk	Soy milk
Water	

Step 2: Add some greens (2 cups OR 1 big handful)

Baby spinach	Kale
Lettuce (butter, red, green, romaine)	Mixed greens
Swiss chard	

Step 3: Add some fruit (about 2 cups)

Apple	Banana
Berries	Grapes
Mango	Orange
Papaya	Peach
Pear	Pineapple

Step 4: Add a superfood or two (optional)

Cacao nibs and powder	Chia seeds
Coconut oil (melted)	Flax seeds (ground)
Hemp seeds	Maca powder
Nut butters	Protein powders
Spirulina	Yogurt

Step 5: Sweeten your smoothie (optional)
This is personal choice. From dates to stevia—it's up to you!

Step 6: Turn on your blender

Step 7: Drink up! Here's to your health!

Invest in Good Equipment

The best ingredients in the world will not do you much good if you do not have the equipment you need to make your smoothies. Aside from (1) some good knives and (2) a cutting board, you will need (3) a high-speed blender. A good blender can make the difference between a smooth, satisfying drink and one that has bits and chunks of vegetables and fruits—not to mention the frustration of trying to drink one through a straw.

Personally, I use a blender attachment for my Bosch kitchen center that I bought 25 years ago. It is powerful and capable of blending and grinding most everything I have put into it and it makes a very nice smoothie. I have never had any problems with it and only had to buy a new set of blades for the very first time about a month ago. It has definitely proven to be worth the investment.

I have recently read that a Blendtec and Vitamix make great blenders that can handle much of what my Bosch does. Some even prefer the Blendtec to the Vitamix. If you plan to incorporate green smoothies into your daily eating plan, you may want to do your own investigation into this area before you invest in a high quality blender.

Here is a short explanation about blenders to help you get started in your research. Blenders appear to come in 3 basic categories, according to their wattages and prices:

- **Lowest:** These are blenders with about 300 watts of power and cost anywhere between $35 to $60 dollars. As a green smoothie maker, they will not last you very long because their motors will burn out.

- **Middle:** Blenders in the mid-range have around 700 watts of power and cost somewhere between $90 and $150. While these blenders have more powerful motors, their motors will also burn out with the heavy-duty use of green smoothie making.

- **Highest:** These are considered commercial-grade blenders and pack a punch of 1100 watts up to 1560. This is where you will find blenders like Blendtec and Vitamix. These are known to last from 15 to 20 years and offer a great warranty.

Some Helpful Blender Tips

If upgrading to a high quality blender is not an option for you right now, I am going to give you some tips on how to make good smoothies—even if your blender is not a super-duper one. With these tips, you should be able to make some delicious smoothies while you save up your dollars to invest in a great blender.

Tip #1 ~ Like I shared with you above, be sure to put the liquid in first. By putting the liquid in first, your blender will create a type of funnel that will help pull the fruit and veggies down into the blades, helping to chop them up better.

Tip #2 ~ Use a sharp knife to cut up your fruits and vegetables. Depending upon the quality of your blender, you may even find it necessary to shred and finely chop your ingredients. This could take you quite a bit of time. *Note: It may be necessary for you to only use fresh or cold fruits in your blender if it is not powerful enough to chop up hard frozen fruits. Also, remove big stems that are found with kale, for example.*

Tip #3 ~ Unlike what I listed above in the chart, you should add the fruit next. This will allow your blender to puree the fruit and help add it to the funnel created by the spinning action. Then when you add the greens, this puree funnel will draw the greens down into the blades, helping to shred and puree them as well.

Tip #4 ~ You will want to make use of various speeds on your blender, as well as using the pulse button if your blender has one. Try working your way up in speeds like this: Use the pulse button a few times, then start on low and work your way up to high over the course of about 30 seconds.

Tip #5 ~ If your blender still has left chunks of fruits and vegetables, consider adding some extra liquid to the blender.

These tips will help you make a green smoothie that will be good in texture, but if you find an opportunity to add a great blender to your wishlist, I think you now know what to look for and what to ask for.

What Greens Should I Use in My Smoothies?

When you stop to think about it, there are so many greens to choose from that can go into your smoothies. Just reflect upon how many greens you see each time you make your way into the produce section of your grocery store. Countless combinations of great tasting (and maybe not so great tasting) smoothies are waiting for your discovery.

Part of why I want you to know how these greens taste in your smoothie is because you want to vary the greens you use. Different greens offer various vitamins, minerals, and other nutrients. As I'm sure you have heard, "Everything in moderation," and green smoothies are no different. Therefore, just tell yourself going into this that you will try different greens and vary the greens you use in your smoothies on a regular basis.

For example, while baby spinach and green leaf lettuce have mild delicate flavors, arugula and kale can be much stronger, even bitter. However, these stronger-flavored greens are often much more nutritious than milder-flavored greens and can provide as much as double the protein and calcium for each cup of juice.

Below you will find a table of numerous greens I put together that you can purchase for your smoothies. This is by no means an exhaustive list. Instead, I have separated them into greens that have a mild flavor when used in your smoothie, and those that are stronger and contribute a peppery or spicy flavor to your drink.

By knowing there is a difference, you can introduce the stronger greens gradually into your drinks by trying one-fourth strong greens with three-fourths mild. As you get a little more adventurous, you can increase the strong greens to half-and-half so your body is able to enjoy the nutrients and variety of flavors the stronger greens offer. Experiment! Delicious flavors are waiting to be discovered by you.

Mild-Tasting Greens	Strong-Tasting Greens
Baby spinach	Arugula
Bok choy	Dandelion greens
Butter lettuce	Endive
Cabbage (red or green)	Kale (large, older leaves)
Collard greens	Mustard greens
Green leaf lettuce	Radicchio
Kale (small, young leaves)	Watercress
Red leaf lettuce	
Romaine lettuce	
Swiss chard	
Sprouts	
Alfalfa sprouts	Chive sprouts
Broccoli sprouts	Mustard sprouts
Mung bean sprouts	Radish sprouts

As you venture into the world of green smoothies or you have enjoyed them for awhile, there is a basic rule to keep in mind: Whenever you see a measurement for greens listed in a recipe, use any combination of that measurement the way you want. If a recipe calls for 2 cups of baby spinach, you can use 1½ cups of baby spinach and ½ cup of kale. Also, consider 1 cup of romaine lettuce and 1 cup of mustard greens.

Mix it up. Create combinations. Be creative! Don't let any smoothie recipe make you feel like you can't experiment. NOBODY has cornered the market on how you have to make a smoothie. You get to decide how much of what ingredient and that's what makes it fun!

Other Vegetables to Experiment with in Your Smoothies

I haven't specifically mentioned this yet, but the fruits and vegetables that are added to your smoothies tend to be raw. Because of this alone, there are many other veggies you can add to your smoothie to add variety and nutrition, however, some are definitely better than others in your smoothies.

I have made a table below of some of the better veggies to use. When non-starchy or low-starchy vegetables are used, you will get better results. In addition, their taste and consistency is better than vegetables with a medium to high starch content.

In addition, vegetables that are high in starch do not combine very well with most fruits so it is best to try and avoid putting them in your smoothie. While they certainly are nutritiously beneficial, their high starchy content can make the consistency of your smoothie undesirable. It is best to eat them raw or in your favorite dishes and soups.

Non- & Low-Starchy Vegetables	Med- & High-Starchy Vegetables
Avocados	Beans
Beets	Corn
Bell peppers (sweet)	Okra
Broccoli	Parsnips
Carrots	Peas
Cauliflower	Potatoes (sweet and white)
Celery	Pumpkin
Cucumbers	Squash
Tomato	Zucchini
	Yams

This chapter should have given you some great ideas for some combinations you could use in your green smoothies. I also tried to include items that are easy to buy at the grocery store or the farmers' market and ones you might already have in your kitchen so you can get started soon.

What Are Some Good Fruits to Use in My Smoothies?

Fruits add natural sweetness and texture to your green smoothies that make them enjoyable and tasty. Greens all by themselves would not taste very good and would be difficult to drink.

There are a few basic guidelines you will want to consider when developing your smoothie because some fruits add a creamy texture while frozen fruits make them....cold!

- Consider fruits that have a lot of juice like watermelon and grapefruit. These could be used to supplement the liquid needed for your smoothie.

- Some fruits add creaminess to your smoothie's consistency, like peaches, mangos, and avocados. They make a good foundational base to your smoothie.

- Others like berries, oranges, and lemons add definitive flavors to your smoothies.

With so many wonderful fruits available, a list would be too long to present here. Instead, I want to give you a few important tips and tricks to help you decide what fruits, and which ones, to include in your smoothies.

Fruit Tips:

1. Decide if the fruit you will be using will also act as a liquid. Watermelons, grapes, grapefruit, and oranges have a lot of fluid in them so you may not need to add as much other liquid as normal.

2. If you desire a creamy texture, use fruits like bananas, peaches, mangos, pears, papaya, and apples.

3. Consider classic fruit combinations that seem to go well together. For example, berries with apples, berries and pineapple, strawberries and bananas, strawberries and peaches, pineapple and mangos. Clearly, these combinations are personal choice, but it is a good way to think about what to add.

4. If your smoothie is finished and it tastes too bitter or strong from the greens, add some flavorful fruits like bananas, berries or pineapple to offset it.

Don't be discouraged if your smoothie doesn't taste quite as wonderful as you were hoping when you put all the ingredients in your blender. That is the nice thing about fruits—you can keep adding them until you get the sweetness you desire. However, be prepared! You will probably end up with more smoothie than you thought. No problem! I will be sharing with you later some tips on how to store your excess smoothie.

What Other Ingredients Can I Add to My Smoothie?

Besides liquids, fruits, and vegetables, I mentioned before that you can add additional ingredients called "superfoods." The best way I can think of to describe a "superfood" is to simply say they are ingredients that have incredible nutrition packed inside them. Including them is an easy and quick way to get nutrients into your body.

Some of you reading this book may simply feel convicted to start eating healthier foods free of pesticides and processed ingredients. If so, then any of the ingredients we have been discussing becomes "superfood" to your body.

Others of you have been eating organically and minimally processed foods for a while so you already know the benefits these "superfoods" bring to your health. If this describes you, then you may be interested in foods that can add an additional boost to the nutritional levels of foods you already enjoy. No matter where you are nutritionally, "superfoods" are taking on a complete identity of their own.

I have to say that the ironic thing to me with all the publicity about superfoods is that many of the ingredients we have talked about that you can include in your green smoothies are considered superfoods! Foods like berries, bananas, greens, broccoli, lemons, and many others are what you use in a green smoothie, so you are already using them.

With that said, I'm only going to list a few items that can be added to your smoothies. These items are slightly more unusual, but easily attainable and not very expensive. These will pack an additional vitamin/mineral punch to your smoothie on top of the ones you receive when using healthy green vegetables and fruits.

Finally, remember that adding superfoods to your smoothie is optional. Like I stated above, drinking green smoothies, especially if you are using fresh ingredients and organic ones on top of that, will offer you many nutrients, antioxidants, and vitamins—even without adding any from this list.

Acai ~ If you thought the taste of chocolate couldn't be good for you, well, think again! Acai berries from Brazil are packed full of antioxidants, fiber, and protein. If you want to include them in your smoothie, add 2 to 3 teaspoons. (Consider grinding them in a small coffee grinder first to create a powder if you have the berries.) They offer a feeling of fullness, creaminess, and lovely chocolaty flavor. Don't be surprised if you suddenly experience some additional energy, too.

Cacao nibs and powder ~ For you chocolate lovers who don't want to feel guilty for enjoying a chocolate shake, incorporate 2 to 3 tablespoons of this delicious powder into your next smoothie. With antioxidants to enhance your immune system, this winning superfood will help you ward off sickness. It is a great source of copper, potassium, zinc, calcium, iron, and magnesium.

By adding 2 to 3 tablespoons of the powder to your smoothie, you will find your cravings for sweets diminish as you enjoy a luscious dessert-like flavor with this superfood.

For a real crunch of chocolate, sprinkle a little bit of the nibs on top of your smoothie, too.

Chia seeds ~ High in omega fatty acids, these little nuggets contain a wide variety of antioxidants, calcium, vitamins, fiber, protein, minerals, and iron. When included in your diet, these seeds will fight heart disease and high cholesterol, but also increase your brain function.

Chia seeds are known to absorb many times their own weight in water. When using them in your smoothie, be sure and consume extra fluids during the day. Some people have experienced constipation because they didn't drink enough fluids. Also, consider only using them occasionally instead of every day or only use half the amount for what is called for in a recipe.

Feel free to add 2 to 3 tablespoons of chia seeds to your smoothie, especially if you would like to thicken its consistency and add a sweeter flavor.

Coconut oil ~ In the past, coconut oil was given a bad rap because of saturated fats. However, it has become known that coconut oil is very beneficial for helping to boost your metabolism. Apparently, the fatty acids found in coconut oil create energy in your body that speeds up your body's ability to burn calories faster. This is especially helpful and nice to know if you are trying to lose weight as part of your green-smoothie plan.

If you want to add a coco-nutty flavor to your smoothie, use about 1 tablespoon of coconut oil and be sure to use the "virgin" coconut oil. However, if you are like me and want to enjoy the benefits of coconut oil without the taste, use oil that doesn't include "virgin" in the title. I find that if I melt it briefly in the microwave so it liquefies and add it near the end of the process, it blends in beautifully.

Flax seeds ~ These highly nutritious seeds are just downright good for you. They supply much needed fiber for eliminating toxins from your digestive system. They help your brain, joints, and immune system fire on all cylinders, and they are good for your heart.

For the best incorporation into your smoothie, be sure to grind them first. However, if you like a slight crunch, you can leave them whole.

Goji berries ~ Looking for a multivitamin in a berry? Well, Goji berries are just the ticket. These little gems pack more than 20 important minerals and vitamins to your smoothie, strengthen your immune system so you can fight off infections, and add valuable amino acids and antioxidants to your diet.

Using between ¼ cup to ½ cup of berries for your smoothie adds sweetness to your drink while adding vitality to your life.

Nuts and nut butters ~ Although nuts are classified as fats, they are also considered superfoods. They offer many different nutrients like antioxidants, minerals, protein, and omega-3 fatty acids. The easiest and smoothest way to incorporate these into your smoothies is to use nut milks like almond and coconut.

Protein powders ~ Protein powders supply added protein to your smoothies. These can provide added nutrients for muscle growth, as well as benefitting your heart. Available in many flavors and dietary options like vegan, raw, and dairy-free, protein powders should be used as directed. While they supply extra protein, they could add unwanted calories.

Spirulina ~ Packed with omega fatty acids and proteins, this fibrous algae is found in the warm alkaline lakes of Africa, Central and South America. It is a rich source of vitamins and minerals and offers super nutrition to your green smoothie.

Consider using between 1 and 2 teaspoons of this powder for a smoothie that packs a punch nutritionally.

Wheatgrass ~ Derived from the wheat plant, wheatgrass is reported to help detoxify your body as well as strengthen your immune system. It is a natural source of magnesium, calcium, iron, and vitamins B-12, E, and A.

Yogurt ~ Plain yogurt added to your smoothie provides smoothness and a slight tartness to your drink. Packed with protein and potassium, yogurt provides healthy bacteria for your intestinal tract, especially when it is enriched with probiotics. If you can tolerate dairy and wish to add a nutritional punch to your smoothie, try adding ½ cup.

Tip: If you decide to use 2 or 3 different superfoods in the same smoothie, consider using half the amounts of each one. For example, if a recipe calls for 3 tablespoons of chia seeds and you want to use flax seeds as well, use 1.5 tablespoons of both chia and flax seeds for a total of 3 tablespoons.

Notes

How to Buy, Clean, Store and Even FREEZE Your Produce

One of the keys to successful smoothie making is to have the ingredients available to you at a moment's notice. When you get the urge for a snack, making a green smoothie can be an easy and quick task if your ingredients are easily accessible and ready to go.

There are two ways to deal with greens once you get them home. You can wash them immediately or you can learn proper ways to store them dry. I have done both of them with success and oftentimes what I choose to do depends upon the time available to me when putting groceries away. My favorite is to put them away without washing them; however, I will wash some greens first if they do not look as perky at home as they looked in the store.

I am going to use this section to walk you through both processes—washing them first and just putting them away. Then I will explain how you can even freeze greens and fruits if you desire.

Washing Your Greens

1. Wash your produce as soon as you get home

Whether you grow your own greens or buy them at the store or farmers' market, wash them as soon as they make it into your kitchen.

- Begin by making sure your sink is clean. Then fill it with water so there is enough room for the leaves to float.

- Remove any rubber bands, twist ties, or other packaging

- Separate the leaves from the stem and cut off any roots from the plants that will not be used in your smoothies

- Place the produce in the water to remove dirt and any little critters you find hiding in the leaves.

2. Dry your produce

Once you are satisfied that your greens are clean, proceed with drying them

- Remove the leaves from the water and allow them to drain in a strainer or colander

- Place clean towels out on your countertops

- Once most of the water has drained from the leaves, spread them out on the towels and pat them dry. You can also use a salad spinner to dry your produce, too.

3. Time to store your greens

Now it is time for you to carefully put away your greens so they are ready for your next smoothies.

- Carefully wrap your greens in dishtowels or paper towels before placing them in plastic bags. This will allow the cloth and paper to absorb condensation and will hasten spoilage

- If storing them in vegetable drawers, line the drawer with paper or cloth so condensation can be absorbed

No-Wash Method for Your Greens

1. Place in the refrigerator

- If your greens got a bath under the showers of the produce section, shake out as much water as possible

- Cut the ends of the stems off

- Line the drawers and containers with a layer of paper towels

- Place your greens in plastic containers that have lids or the drawers in your refrigerator, making sure the ends are facing the back of the refrigerator. This will prevent the delicate leafy parts of your produce from freezing because it is coldest at the back of your refrigerator

- Now put paper towels on top of the greens (If your greens are moist, place paper towels in between some of the layers of the greens to absorb moisture)

- Close the drawer or place the lid on your plastic containers and you are done

- When it comes time to use your greens, just run each leaf under the faucet to remove any dirt, shake off the water, then place in your blender

  I want to note a couple of things here about using each method:

- If you don't like to clean your sink very often or are worried about germs, I would encourage you to use the no-wash method

- Washing greens and letting them dry is definitely time consuming. If you don't have the time, learn to put them away using the no-wash method

- Whatever method you use, greens will start to wilt anywhere from three to five days after you bring them home. Strive to buy the "perkiest" greens you can find at the store to keep them from wilting as long as possible.

Freezing Your Greens

This trick was one of the best things I learned several years ago that has saved me so much money. It allows you to buy your greens in bulk, especially when they are on sale, and they will keep for months in your freezer. This means that you can always have the ingredients you need for a smoothie, anytime you want one.

There are a couple of ways to freeze your greens.

1. If you are buying them from the produce section and they have not been pre-washed, then you should plan to bring them home, wash them, dry them, break them into reasonably sized leaf pieces, then either place them on a tray or cookie sheet and put into your freezer or put them into a large freezer plastic bag. While placing them onto a tray is not necessary, it does prevent the possibilities of the leaves freezing together into one big lump.

   - If you freeze them on a tray, then once the leaves are frozen, lift them off the tray and place in a freezer bag. Then when you are ready for a smoothie, just place several leaves in the blender and process with your other ingredients. (It may be necessary to add additional liquid when using frozen greens.)

2. My favorite way to freeze greens is to buy them at the store, already pre-washed, chopped and in big bags, and then come home and throw the whole thing in the freezer. This saves so much time and is often very cost effective.

Why freeze greens?

1. I like frosty smoothies the best so using frozen ingredients in my smoothies really pleases my taste buds.
2. If you buy organic greens at the store or farmers' market, then you can have healthy greens any time of year—even when they are not in season.

3. Freezing greens can save you a bunch of money. If your greens start out in the refrigerator but you don't get around to using them before they start to wilt, you don't have to throw them away. Freeze them and enjoy them later.

4. When you freeze your greens, they become brittle so they are actually easier to crunch up and jam

5. A tip I recently discovered was taking greens and blending them with some water so they are pourable. Then pour the liquid into ice cube trays, freeze, then pop them into a freezer bag. When it comes time to make my smoothie, just add four or five cubes. You can also do this with fruits like oranges, apples, and pears—so many different ones. It's so easy!

Freezing Your Fruits

Freezing fruits is a great way to enjoy your favorites all year long—even when they are not in season. The nice part about this is your fruits will keep nicely in the freezer for as long as a year.

Here are a few of things you will need to do to prepare your fruits for freezing. Not hard—just necessary.

- **Bananas** ~ Peel the skin off, then place in a freezer bag side by side, one layer thick. They are easier to separate when it comes time to use them than if you pile them on top of each other.

- **Strawberries** ~ Remove the tops and cut in half. Place on a tray with a lip in a single layer and then freeze. Once frozen, place in a freezer bag.

- **Mangos** ~ Peel and slice into chunks or slices. Place on a tray with a lip in a single layer and then freeze. Once frozen, place in a freezer bag.

- **Blueberries, blackberries, raspberries** ~ Place on a tray with a lip in a single layer and then freeze. Once frozen, place in a freezer bag.

- **Pineapple** ~ Remove the rind and cut into chunks. Place on a tray with a lip in a single layer and then freeze. Once frozen, place in a freezer bag.

Feel free to experiment with other fruits like oranges and melons. Even if some of them do not turn out exactly the way you thought, at least you will know what works for you.

Notes

TIPS AND TRICKS OF GREEN SMOOTHIE MAKING

Helpful Tips and Tricks

This chapter is full of helpful tips and tricks that will enable you to make great tasting smoothies. You will even learn how you can salvage a smoothie that doesn't turn out quite as you expected.

I have divided these tips and tricks into different aspects of green smoothie making. They are:

- Ingredients

- Temperatures, liquids, and ice

- Storing

- Taste

- Texture

- Other comments

Feel free to skip to the section you are most interested in or simply read through all of them.

Ingredients

- You have probably heard the saying, "Everything in moderation." Well, this applies to the greens you use in your smoothies, too. To avoid some of the discomforts you can experience when drinking green smoothies, such as bloating, rotate and vary the greens you use in your smoothies occasionally. Eating many of the same raw greens in your smoothies on a regular basis can lead to digestive issues.

- When using fruit in your smoothie, think of mango, banana, and pear as the "base" of your smoothie. Then choose a flavorful fruit like berries, oranges, and pineapple to complement your base. Thinking of fruit in your smoothies like this will give you great freedom in experimenting and achieving good-tasting results.

- To keep the calories and sugar content down in your smoothies, add just enough fruit to make them sweet enough to enjoy but not too sweet to make them calorie-dense.

- Eating the same greens repeatedly will cheat your body out of valuable nutrition variety offers.

- When using coconut oil in your smoothie (I prefer the unflavored kind in mine), melt it briefly so it goes from a solid to a liquid. Then add to your smoothie near the end of the process. This ensures that it will blend in smoothly with your ingredients.

- If you use seeds in your smoothies, ground them to a powder first. I do this using a small coffee mill devoted to grinding my seeds.

- For added protein, put a scoop of your favorite protein powder to your smoothie at the end, blend briefly and enjoy! (I don't like a foamy smoothie so I blend in the powder just until it is dissolved into the liquid.) Protein powders also add some sweetness to your drinks.

- Give your smoothie a fresh taste by adding some parsley or mint leaves.

- To enhance the nutritious value of a smoothie, use fresh juices instead of canned or processed ingredients.

- Adding a bunch of different ingredients can make your smoothie taste bland by disguising the flavors, so keep it simple.

- When you use citrus in your smoothies, you want to peel the rind off completely before adding them. If you don't, it will cause your smoothie to taste bitter.

- Unlike citrus, you can leave thinner peelings on the fruit and add to your smoothie. Ingredients like grapes, pears, apples, and even carrots will not mess up the taste of your smoothie and will add some extra fiber, too.

- When using greens that have a bite to them and are rather spicy, think about using sweet and flavorful fruits like bananas, berries, and pineapples to smooth out the bitterness.

- If you do not like bananas in your smoothie, try adding ingredients like avocados, mangos, and peaches. These denser fruits will give you a smooth texture like bananas.

Temperatures, liquids, and ice

- If you are using room temperature fruit in your smoothie, you may find you want it colder. If so, just add some ice cubes or frozen berries to give your smoothie a more satisfying temperature.

- Sometimes your smoothie will be too thick. If so, just add a little water to improve its consistency or a piece of juicy fruit like an orange.

- **Start all your smoothies with at least a cup of liquid.** Try using nut milks like coconut or almond, rice milk, orange juice, or just plain water. Soy milk is an option but I tend not to use it because soy has not been rating very high on the nutritional scales lately.

- If you know you are going to add ice to make a cold smoothie, use flavorful fruits in your smoothie. Sometimes ice cubes can give you a watered-down taste.

- If you have too much smoothie left over after drinking your fill, consider making popsicles out of the leftovers. Depending upon what you put into your smoothie, it may be even delicious enough that your kids will enjoy your popsicles, too.

- Consider making a smoothie and heating it up to eat it as a soup.

- Whenever you want a smoothie that is cold and frosty, use frozen fruit instead of room temperature fruit. If it gets too frozen looking and your mixture doesn't appear to be blending, just add some extra liquid slowly until the smoothie begins to show a funnel rotating in the middle.

Storing

- Smoothies can be made ahead of time, but are best nutritionally if you drink them within 24 hours. If you have some leftover or you want to make one the night before to enjoy at breakfast, store in an airtight container in your refrigerator.

- I like to use plastic quart-sized canning jars with plastic lids to keep extra smoothie drink airtight. These also make it very easy to shake the smoothie back together before drinking.

Taste

- The best thing to do before pouring your smoothie into your glass is to stick your finger in and taste your creation. (Okay, use a spoon instead.) This gives you a chance to add sweetness and additional fruits, ice, etc. for improved flavor.

- If you are new to green smoothies, stay with mild-tasting greens for a while. Give your taste buds some time to get used to drinking your vegetables, then add some stronger greens when you think you are ready.

- ==Too sweet?== Add a pinch of salt, some extra greens or some celery to calm down the sweetness. Alternatively, try adding ¼ teaspoon of lemon.

- ==Too bitter?== Add sweet and flavorful fruits like pineapple, berries, oranges, and bananas. If you are okay with added sweeteners, try stevia, raw honey, or pure maple syrup. In addition, dried fruits like apricots, peaches, and cherries are wonderful, too.

- ==Too sour?== Try adding something to sweeten your drink. Grapes, mangos, pears and bananas often work as well as an added sweetener.

- Don't be afraid to experiment. If you end up with a flop you just can't figure out how to fix, you could use it as a soup base for your next creation.

Texture

- Want a smoothie that is creamy? Try adding some avocado.

- If your blender doesn't make your smoothies smooth, chew your smoothie instead. From a nutritional standpoint, this is actually a good thing. Because the release of the enzyme, amylase, begins in your mouth when you chew your food, chewing bits and pieces of fruits and vegetables in your smoothie can actually increase some of the nutritional value you receive from your smoothie.

- Adding ingredients like protein powders can change the texture of your smoothie.

- Frozen fruits and greens will make your smoothie thick and cold (my favorite).

Other comments

- While I really like a nice, cold, even icy smoothie, I have tried to learn to drink them slower. Recently, I learned that taking a few extra moments to mix my mouthful of smoothie with some saliva will actually help my body digest more of the nutrients in the green smoothies I drink—and isn't that one of the biggest reasons why we drink them?

- While I enjoy making my own juices, smoothies are much easier for me. Just throw the ingredients into the blender, process, pour, then rinse out the blender and I'm done. This is so much easier to do than cleaning the juice extractor after I use it.

- I confess. I like to use orange juice in my smoothies. It is a high quality orange juice and yes, I know all the literature says that this is a lot of carbohydrates and increases the sugar content, but that's what I like. I have certainly used coconut milk, water, coconut water, and even yogurt as my liquid, but orange juice is still my favorite.

Let's Drink! Recipes for a Great Tasting Green Smoothie

It is finally time to pull out your blender, gather your ingredients and make yourself a green smoothie! I have equipped you with everything you need to know except some recipes to help you tie it all together.

As we have covered before, there are a few basic steps to follow as demonstrated in the chart called, "Steps for Creating a Green Smoothie." To simplify this technique even more, all you have to do is:

- Put your liquid in the bottom

- Add your fruit and greens

- Blend things up

- Taste to make sure you like it, pour it into a glass, and drink!

For the recipes that follow, I will not be including the directions each time because they are all pretty much the same process; however,

I will list the ingredients for the smoothie in the order you would add them—liquid, then greens, etc.

If I think of something specific or have a tip to offer, I will make it following the ingredients used for that particular smoothie.

It is difficult to say how many servings each recipe makes but they certainly make at least one. Several things come into play when making a smoothie:

- You may not be quite as hungry as you thought you were so you have some extra left over to share or keep for another serving

- Fruits and "handfuls" vary in size so you may end up with more smoothie in your recipe than I would in mine if we were using the exact same ingredients. For example, if my banana and apples are smaller than yours, you will end up with more smoothie than me.

- If you do not like the texture of your smoothie, you may decide to add additional fruits, liquid, or ice.

- Over time, you will be able to guestimate with pretty good accuracy how much a smoothie makes by the amounts you add to your blender.

Now, let's get started!

SMOOTHIE RECIPES

New Beginnings Smoothie

If this is the first time you have ever tried making a green smoothie, this is a delicious way to begin.

- 1 cup nut milk (coconut or almond)
- 2 cups baby spinach
- 2 cups frozen fruit (combination of mango and pineapple is really good)
- 1 scoop protein powder

I like to mix up the first three ingredients until they are thoroughly combined. Then, I add the scoop of protein powder, blend until it is just mixed in and then stop. This keeps the foaming action of the powder minimal.

Simple Smoothie

Here is another recipe that is simple and tasty.

- 1 cup coconut water
- 2 cups mixed greens
- 2 cups mixed berries, frozen
- 1 scoop protein powder

Polynesian Smoothie

- 1 cup coconut water
- 1 big handful mixed greens
- 1 cup mango chunks, frozen
- 1 cup pineapple chunks, frozen
- ¾ cup Greek yogurt

Spicy Raspberry Smoothie

- 1½ cups nut milk (coconut or almond)
- 1 cup baby spinach
- 1 cup arugula
- 1 cup fresh raspberries, frozen
- 4 strawberries, frozen
- ½ teaspoon vanilla extract

Fruity Spinach Smoothie

- 1 cup water (tap or filtered)
- 2 cups baby spinach
- 2 cups frozen mixed berries
- 2 tablespoons ground flax seeds (optional)
- 1 teaspoon honey or maple syrup

Orangana Pear Smoothie

- 1 cup orange juice
- 1 cup kale
- 1 cup baby spinach
- 1 pear with core and stem removed, but skin left on
- 1 large banana, frozen

Green Goddess Smoothie

- 1½ nut milk (coconut or almond)
- 1 large kale leaf (or 1 cup shredded kale)
- 1 small handful baby spinach
- 1 large banana
- 2 cups pineapple chunks
- 1 scoop protein powder

Frosty Green Smoothie

- 1 cup nut milk (coconut or almond)
- 2 cups shredded kale
- 2 frozen bananas
- 1 avocado
- 3 teaspoons ground flax seed
- 2 teaspoons honey or pure maple syrup

Sweet Goodness Smoothie

- 1 cup water
- 1 cup orange juice
- 2 cups baby spinach
- 1 cup mango chunks
- 1 cup pineapple chunks
- 2 medium bananas OR 1 large banana

Nutty Green Smoothie

- 1½ cups nut milk (almond or coconut)
- 2 cups baby spinach
- 2 bananas
- 2 cups grapes
- ¼ cup almond butter

Bunny's Favorite Smoothie

- 1½ cups water
- 1 big handful baby spinach
- 2 carrots, cut into chunks
- 1 banana
- 1 cup mango chunks
- 1 cup pineapple chunks

Green Coconut Smoothie

- 1½ cups coconut water
- 1 cup baby spinach
- 1 cup spring mix OR mixed greens
- 1 banana
- 2 cups pineapple chunks
- ½ cup unsweetened coconut
- 2 tablespoons coconut oil, melted

Berry Good Smoothie

- ½ cup water
- 1 large orange, peeled
- 1 large handful baby spinach
- 6 large frozen strawberries
- ½ cup Greek yogurt
- In this recipe, blend the water and orange together first to make your liquid.

CinnaPear Smoothie

- 1½ cups nut milk (coconut or almond)
- 1 big handful baby spinach
- 1 large banana
- 4 pears, core removed but skin left on
- 1 teaspoon cinnamon
- 1 scoop of your favorite protein powder

Feel free to make this a frozen banana. Or try 2 bananas and 3 pears to change it up.

Green Pines Smoothie

- 1½ cups coconut water
- 1 handful baby spinach
- 2 cups pineapple chunks (really good when these are frozen)
- 1 avocado, seeded and skinned

If you use frozen pineapple chunks, you may have to add a little more coconut water.

Nutty Banana Smoothie

- 1½ cups orange juice
- 1 cup baby spinach
- 1 cup mustard greens
- 1 banana, frozen
- 1 pear with skin on, cored
- 2 tablespoons almond butter

Dark and Delicious Smoothie

- 1½ cups water or coconut water
- 1 big handful baby spinach
- 1 cup blackberries
- 1 cup pitted cherries
- 1 banana
- 1 scoop protein powder

Applelicious Smoothie

- ¾ cup coconut water
- 1 cucumber, peeled
- 1 large handful spring mix OR mixed greens
- 1 kale leaf
- 1 celery stalk
- 1 large frozen banana
- 1 medium sweet apple with skin on, cored
- 2 tablespoons lemon juice

Blend the coconut water and cucumber first to make your liquid.

CocoPiney Smoothie

- 1½ cups coconut water
- 3 kale leaves
- 1 large banana
- 2 cups frozen pineapple chunks
- 1/8 cup coconut oil, melted

Smoothy Smoothie

- 1 cup orange juice
- 1 kale leaf
- 1 small handful baby spinach
- 1 banana, frozen
- 1 pear with skin on, cored
- 1 tablespoon ground flax seed

Berry Springy Smoothie

- - 1 cup nut milk (coconut or almond)
- - 2 cups spring mix OR mixed greens
- - 1 peach, seeded
- - ½ cup raspberries
- - 4 large frozen strawberries
- - 1 scoop protein powder

Apple Peary Smoothie

- ¾ cup coconut water
- 1 cucumber, peeled
- 1 medium apple with skin on, cored
- 2 pears with skin on, cored
- 1 cup chopped cilantro
- ½ cup Greek yogurt

Red Chalet Smoothie

- 1 cup orange juice
- 1 cup chopped Swiss chard
- 1 cup mango chunks, frozen
- 5 whole strawberries, frozen
- ¾ cup Greek yogurt

Refreshing Raspberry Smoothie

- 1 cup coconut milk
- 1 big handful romaine leaves
- 2 cups strawberries
- ½ cup fresh mint, chopped
- 2 tablespoons honey
- 1 scoop protein powder

Luscious Pink Smoothie

- 1 cup nut milk (coconut or almond)
- 1 big handful romaine
- 1 cup mango chunks, frozen
- 5 large strawberries, frozen
- 1 cup pineapple chunks, frozen

Purple Passion Smoothie

- 1½ cups coconut water
- 2 cups mixed greens
- 1 medium banana
- 1 cup berries (blueberries, blackberries, raspberries, etc.)
- 1 cup pitted cherries (I love bing cherries)
- 2 tablespoons flaxseed, ground

Hawaiian Smoothie

- 1 cup nut milk (coconut or almond)
- 2 cups mixed greens
- 1 banana
- 1 avocado
- 1 cucumber, peeled
- 2 cups seedless grapes
- 1 cup pineapple chunks
- ¼ cup coconut flakes

Grapes Nuts Smoothie

- 1 cup nut milk (coconut or almond)
- 1 orange, peeled
- 2 cups bok choy, chopped
- 2 large bananas
- 2 cups seedless grapes
- ¼ cup almond butter

Blend the nut milk and orange together first to make the liquid.

Blueberry Delight Smoothie

- - 1 cup nut milk (coconut or almond)
- - 2 cups chopped Swiss chard
- - 1 cup mango chunks, frozen
- - 1 cup blueberries, frozen
- - ¾ cup Greek yogurt
- - 2 tablespoons coconut oil, melted

Mixed Up Smoothie

- 1½ cups coconut water
- 1 cup baby spinach
- 1 cup mustard greens, chopped
- 1 apple with skin on, cored
- 1 cup mixed berries, frozen
- 1 cup pineapple chunks, frozen
- 1 scoop protein powder (optional)

Green Banana Smoothie

- 1 cup nut milk (coconut or almond)
- ½ orange juice
- 1 large kale leaf
- 1 frozen banana
- 1 cup frozen pineapple chunks
- 1 tablespoon coconut oil

Green Refreshment Smoothie

- 1 cup nut milk (coconut or almond)
- 1 large kale leaf
- 1 cucumber, peeled
- 1 banana
- 1 cup pineapple chunks
- 1 cup red grapes
- ½ avocado

Blue Heaven Smoothie

- 1 cup orange juice
- 1 big handful red or green leaf lettuce
- 2 small bananas
- 1 cup blueberries
- 1 cup strawberries
- 1 teaspoon spirulina powder

Index of Main Ingredients in Recipes

To help you find recipes by ingredients, I have organized an index section you can use which is organized by the main ingredients used in each smoothie. Simply look for an ingredient you might have on hand, read the name of the recipe listed under that ingredient, see which page it is listed on, and it will take you to that recipe.

Note: As I have shared throughout this book, I will stress it one last time: **If you find a recipe you want to try but do not have some specific ingredients, just substitute with something comparable.** For example, use water instead of nut milks; use romaine instead of baby spinach; use peaches instead of bananas. Experiment! Some of my best smoothies were ones I made up with what I had in my kitchen.

~ apple

Applelicious Smoothie	62
Apple Peary Smoothie	64
Mixed Up Smoothie	67

~ avocado

Frosty Green Smoothie	57
Green Pines Smoothie	60
Hawaiian Smoothie	66
Green Refreshment Smoothie	68

~ banana

Orangana Pear Smoothie	56
Green Goddess Smoothie	57
Frosty Green Smoothie	57
Sweet Goodness Smoothie	57
Nutty Green Smoothie	58
Bunny's Favorite Smoothie	58
Green Coconut Smoothie	58
Green Pines Smoothie	60
Nutty Banana Smoothie	60
Dark and Delicious Smoothie	61
Applelicious Smoothie	62
CocoPiney Smoothie	62
Smoothy Smoothie	63
Purple Passion Smoothie	65
Hawaiian Smoothie	66
Grapes Nuts Smoothie	66
Green Banana Smoothie	68
Green Refreshment Smoothie	68
Blue Heaven Smoothie	68

~ blackberries

Dark and Delicious Smoothie	61

~ blueberries

Blueberry Delight Smoothie	67
Blue Heaven Smoothie	68

~ Bok choy

Grapes Nuts Smoothie	66

~ carrot

Bunny's Favorite Smoothie	58

~ celery

Applelicious Smoothie	62

~ cherries

Bunny's Favorite Smoothie	58
Dark and Delicious Smoothie	61

~ coconut water

Simple Smoothie	55
Polynesian Smoothie	55
Green Coconut Smoothie	58
Bunny's Favorite Smoothie	58
CinnaPear Smoothie	60
Dark and Delicious Smoothie	61
Applelicious Smoothie	62
CocoPiney Smoothie	62
Apple Peary Smoothie	64
Mixed Up Smoothie	67

~ cucumber

Applelicious Smoothie	62
Apple Peary Smoothie	64
Hawaiian Smoothie	66
Green Refreshment Smoothie	68

~ frozen fruit

New Beginnings Smoothie	54
Simple Smoothie	55
Polynesian Smoothie	55
Spicy Raspberry Smoothie	55
Fruity Spinach Smoothie	56
Berry Good Smoothie	59
Berry Springy Smoothie	63
Luscious Pink Smoothie	65

~ grapes

Nutty Green Smoothie	58
Hawaiian Smoothie	66
Grapes Nuts Smoothie	66
Green Refreshment Smoothie	68

~ green leaf lettuce

Blue Heaven Smoothie	68

~ kale

Orangana Pear Smoothie	56
Green Goddess Smoothie	57
Frosty Green Smoothie	57
Applelicious Smoothie	62

CocoPiney Smoothie	62
Smoothy Smoothie	63
Green Banana Smoothie	68
Green Refreshment Smoothie	68

~ mango

Polynesian Smoothie	55
Sweet Goodness Smoothie	57
Bunny's Favorite Smoothie	58
Red Chalet Smoothie	64
Luscious Pink Smoothie	65
Blueberry Delight Smoothie	67

~ mixed berries

Simple Smoothie	55
Fruity Spinach Smoothie	56
Bunny's Favorite Smoothie	58
Mixed Up Smoothie	67

~ mixed greens

Simple Smoothie	55
Polynesian Smoothie	55
Bunny's Favorite Smoothie	58
Green Coconut Smoothie	58
Applelicious Smoothie	62
Berry Springy Smoothie	63
Hawaiian Smoothie	66

~ mustard greens

Nutty Banana Smoothie	60
Mixed Up Smoothie	67

~ nut milk

New Beginnings Smoothie	54
Spicy Raspberry Smoothie	55
Green Goddess Smoothie	57
Frosty Green Smoothie	57
Nutty Green Smoothie	58
CinnaPear Smoothie	60
Berry Springy Smoothie	63
Refreshing Strawberry Smoothie	64
Luscious Pink Smoothie	65
Hawaiian Smoothie	66
Grapes Nuts Smoothie	66
Blueberry Delight Smoothie	67
Green Banana Smoothie	68
Green Refreshment Smoothie	68

~ orange/orange juice

Orangana Pear Smoothie	56
Sweet Goodness Smoothie	57
Berry Good Smoothie	59
Nutty Banana Smoothie	60
Smoothy Smoothie	63
Red Chalet Smoothie	64
Grapes Nuts Smoothie	66
Green Banana Smoothie	68
Blue Heaven Smoothie	68

~ peaches

Berry Springy Smoothie	63

~ pears

Orangana Pear Smoothie	56
CinnaPear Smoothie	60
Nutty Banana Smoothie	60
Smoothy Smoothie	63
Apple Peary Smoothie	64

~ pineapple

Polynesian Smoothie	55
Green Goddess Smoothie	57
Sweet Goodness Smoothie	57
Bunny's Favorite Smoothie	58
Green Coconut Smoothie	58
Green Pines Smoothie	60
CocoPiney Smoothie	62
Luscious Pink Smoothie	65
Hawaiian Smoothie	66
Mixed Up Smoothie	67
Green Banana Smoothie	68
Green Refreshment Smoothie	68

~ raspberries

Spicy Raspberry Smoothie	55
Berry Springy Smoothie	63

~ red leaf lettuce

Blue Heaven Smoothie	68

~ Romaine lettuce

Refreshing Strawberry Smoothie	64
Luscious Pink Smoothie	65

~ spinach

New Beginnings Smoothie	54
Spicy Raspberry Smoothie	55
Fruity Spinach Smoothie	56
Orangana Pear Smoothie	56
Green Goddess Smoothie	57
Sweet Goodness Smoothie	57
Nutty Green Smoothie	58
Bunny's Favorite Smoothie	58
Green Coconut Smoothie	58
Berry Good Smoothie	59
CinnaPear Smoothie	60
Green Pines Smoothie	60
Nutty Banana Smoothie	60
Dark and Delicious Smoothie	61
Smoothy Smoothie	63
Berry Springy Smoothie	63
Mixed Up Smoothie	67

~ strawberries

Spicy Raspberry Smoothie	55
Berry Good Smoothie	59
Red Chalet Smoothie	64
Refreshing Strawberry Smoothie	64
Luscious Pink Smoothie	65
Blue Heaven Smoothie	68

~ Superfoods (nuts, nut butters, seeds, protein powder, yogurt, etc. and always optional)

New Beginnings Smoothie	54
Simple Smoothie	55

Polynesian Smoothie	55
Fruity Spinach Smoothie	56
Green Goddess Smoothie	57
Frosty Green Smoothie	57
Nutty Green Smoothie	58
Green Coconut Smoothie	58
Berry Good Smoothie	59
CinnaPear Smoothie	60
Nutty Banana Smoothie	60
Dark and Delicious Smoothie	61
CocoPiney Smoothie	62
Berry Springy Smoothie	63
Apple Peary Smoothie	64
Red Chalet Smoothie	64
Refreshing Strawberry Smoothie	64
Hawaiian Smoothie	66
Grapes Nuts Smoothie	66
Blueberry Delight Smoothie	67
Mixed Up Smoothie	67
Blue Heaven Smoothie	68

~ Swiss chard

Red Chalet Smoothie	64
Blueberry Delight Smoothie	67

About Jennifer Wells

Always into sports and very active growing up, Jennifer never gave much thought to diet and exercise. Weight gain was not much of an issue. Then, after marriage and the birth of her twin boys, Jennifer noticed she had problems keeping her weight under control.

After numerous years of frustration, trying to get rid of stubborn pounds and not feeling as well as she wanted, Jennifer began her own personal research into diet and exercise. As a result, she ended up going back to school to get a degree in nutritional science.

Now she enjoys living a healthy lifestyle, spending time outdoors, teaching classes on nutrition at her local high school, and sharing healthy tips and information with family and friends.

And just in case you were curious, Jennifer is now back down to her weight before she had her four children.

Made in the USA
San Bernardino, CA
06 December 2013